Profitable Businesses

for

Notaries, Entrepreneurs, and

Entrepreneur Wannabes

Refreshed Edition

Theresa Cyrus

Published by The Pereleong Group LLC
Virginia Beach, VA

ISBN (Print): **979-8-9991297-0-3**
ISBN (eBook): **979-8-9991297-1-0**

Edition: Refreshed — AI-Proof Profitable Businesses 2025
Cover: T.J. Ferrell

Printed in the United States of America

For my daughters Aziza, Sakile, Asha and Amira

and for Tanty.

Acknowledgments

The village concept is alive and well, but some of the names have changed. Thank you Je'Nein, John, Oriolla, Samantha and Shannell. Your contributions are immeasurable.

TABLE OF CONTENTS

Foreword

For most of my life, the rules of entrepreneurship remained largely unchanged. I started my first business almost 25 years ago, and for more than a decade, the landscape barely shifted. Not anymore. Today, the world of business moves at the speed of light. Technology—especially artificial intelligence (AI)—has added a new layer of uncertainty. Security and profitability can feel elusive.

Profitable Businesses for Notaries, Entrepreneurs, and Entrepreneur Wannabes introduces readers to a variety of businesses with startup costs everyday people can afford that are AI-proof.... It included suggestions submitted by readers. This book provides a roadmap that is just as valuable to the seasoned notary as it is to the entrepreneurial "wannabe."

I've lived this journey. Over two decades as a signing agent, I've completed more than 10,000 signings. I've owned and built a successful commercial cleaning franchise, and I continue to speak, and mentor budding entrepreneurs who are ready to step into business ownership.

With the help of my readers' feedback, this second edition goes even further. You'll find clear definitions, more real-world examples, stories from established entrepreneurs, and much more.

So, grab a pen, take plenty of notes, and let's get to work. Your profitable business journey starts NOW.

P.S. This is a bit of a "How To Use This Book".

I've included Note pages every 2-3 chapters so that you can jot down your thoughts quickly. Ask yourself, "What aspects of the business do I like?", "What aspects DON'T I like?". "What aspects of the business am I good at?",

"What aspects of the business would I have a steep learning curve with?". Also, use the pages to record what questions are coming up for you that will fuel your research.

Chapter 1: My Story

Ive been a Notary Public since July 2001. At one time, I held commissions in New York and Virginia while splitting my life and work between them.

How did it begin? My landlady knocked on my door after a refinance and said, "This lady came to my house and did my refinance—she said it's easy to do and the money is good." At the time I was a single mom of three under eight and pregnant with my fourth. "Easy and good" sounded like manna from the heavens.

I called the "lady"—**Yolanda Mozejko**—who explained she was a loan signing agent, guiding borrowers through loan documents for title companies and lenders. She led me step by step through the process until I was commissioned and confident enough to handle signings on my own. I'm no longer in touch with her, but I'm forever grateful. That training changed my family's life.

Since my first signing in September 2001, I've completed more than **10,000** signings—refinances, HELOCs, purchases, reverse mortgages (HECMs), loan modifications, and more. In my best year I earned well over **$100,000** and had the freedom to shape my schedule. I typically worked 8 a.m.–8 p.m., Monday–Friday, with most signings after the 15th— leaving plenty of early-month days for the beach with my kids. Along the way, I trained others who built successful businesses of their own.

I later expanded into merchant verifications, trusted enrollments, and field inspections, and even explored wedding officiating. In 2021, with my children grown, I stepped back from loan signings, but I continue to perform collateral inspections. These days, I'm all about exploration— of myself, new places, and new projects—being of service, and savoring time with those I love.

My notary commission continues to be a source of pride and possibility. May it open doors for you as well.

Chapter 2: Becoming a Notary Public (for Entrepreneurs, and Entrepreneur Wannabes)

A notary helps prevent fraud by serving as an impartial witness. Notaries verify the signer's identity, and establishes their willingness to sign, and understanding of what they are signing.

Generally, people interested in becoming a notary, must meet the following requirements:

1) Be at least 18 years old

2) Reside in the state where they are going to be commissioned, or live in a nearby state where there is a reciprocal relationship. That is, the nearby states have a mutual agreement that allows their residents certain privileges.

3) Pass a background check

4) Complete any requisite educational training.

Notes

Chapter 3: Mobile Notary Public

One of the simplest and most popular businesses for notaries public is providing mobile notary services. A mobile notary is a notary public who travels to meet clients in person to perform notarial services. Instead of requiring individuals to come to a fixed location like an office or bank, a mobile notary goes to the client's location. This service is often used for convenience, especially for individuals who may have difficulty traveling or arranging transportation.

Clients who have utilized my mobile notary services include nursing home patients, hospital patients, new moms, housebound individuals, people traveling very soon, and those who need notary services after hours. Other sources of clients include, but are not limited to independent living communities, tow yards, places of worship, transitional living facilities, correctional facilities, acute care, and rehabilitation facilities. Notaries are also able to secure contracts with the federal government worth thousands of dollars, we explore that opportunity in more depth in Chapter 12: Working With the Federal Government.

Documents that often require notarization include but are not limited to automobile, business, healthcare proxies, medical, power of attorneys, real estate, structured settlements, subpoenas, trusts, and wills.

While states limit what a notary can charge per notarization, many states allow the notary to set the cost to travel to the client and perform the service. The states that regulate the amount the notary charges often follow the I.R.S. guidelines or set an amount based on the time it takes to travel. Some states limit the amount a notary can charge for mobile services, so check with your state to establish what is allowed.

When I began, my base fee for traveling to a customer was $50, it varied according to the distance I traveled, the time of day (or night), and the scope of the services I was being asked to provide. I once met with a client at 5 am so that they could make their early morning flight, and I have done signings as late as 1 am when needed.

My services were listed on numerous signing company websites and websites such as Craigslist, and Nextdoor (the social network for neighborhoods across the country). I also got clients by referral. I've seen people advertise their services with a magnetic sign attached to their car doors. Online advertising is a valuable option as well. Google business pages are an effective way to promote a business, and it's FREE!

1) Irregular Income - The income from notary work can be irregular, especially when you are just starting. Building a client base takes time, and your earnings may fluctuate seasonally or with market demand.

2) Travel Expenses and Time - As a mobile notary, you will need to travel to your clients, which can add up in terms of time and expenses for fuel, vehicle maintenance, and possibly parking fees.

3) Depending on your area, there might be significant competition, including from other mobile notaries and electronic notarization services, which could impact your ability to secure clients.

Chapter 4: Loan/ Notary Signing Agent

The terms Notary Signing Agent (NSA) and Loan Signing Agent (LSA) are used interchangeably and refer to what is possibly the best-known, and one of the more lucrative business opportunities for American notaries, particularly in areas with a high volume of real estate transactions. s

NSAs are notaries who are contracted by title companies, mortgage lenders, or signing services to ensure that loan documents are properly executed by the signers. Proper execution means ensuring that all the necessary documents are completely and properly signed, initialed, and dated by the borrower AND you, and notarized by you. These documents may include but are not limited to the numerous and often specific refinance, purchase, home equity line, reverse mortgage, commercial, and loan modification documents. In most instances, you will provide the borrower with a complete copy of the unsigned loan package. Speak with your client to determine if they will permit you to do double-sided copies or partial copies, or will allow you to email the borrower a copy of the loan package.

Several states require the notary to work under the supervision of an attorney or obtain a professional license. As of the writing of this book, the attorney states include Connecticut, Delaware, Georgia, Massachusetts, North Carolina, South Carolina, Vermont, and West Virginia. Professional licenses are required in Indiana, Maryland, Minnesota, Vermont, and Virginia (if money is received or handled at the closing). Do your research to determine in what capacity you are authorized to perform loan signings in your state.

Before we delve further into becoming an NSA, let's clarify the differences between being a NSA and a Certified NSA. A

Notary Signing Agent is a Notary Public who has received the basic additional training or expertise required for handling loan document signings, such as how to secure the borrower's privacy. This is training that can be obtained through self-study.

A Certified Notary Signing Agent has undergone a higher level of training (and testing) by a reputable company to certify that they have been vetted, and can competently handle a variety of loan documents. Since the 2008 financial/real estate crisis, there has been a push for notaries who wish to perform loan signings to be certified, which while certainly helpful, is not mandatory. However, these courses may provide additional education and resources to enhance a Notary Signing Agent's skills and knowledge in conducting loan signings.

On average, the fee for a typical loan signing can range from $75-$200, based on the number of pages and the complexity of the signing. Purchases, refinances, and reverse mortgages generally take significantly longer than equity lines and loan modifications, so it's reasonable to charge more for the time taken. There are instances where you can receive several hundred dollars for a closing if there are extenuating circumstances. A colleague of mine was once paid $400 for her and her husband to travel by ferry to an island to perform a signing.

An LSA can grow their business to handle hundreds of signings every month. At the height of my business, I was performing approximately 125 refinances and home equity lines per month and earning approximately $10-12,000.

Special Considerations (Pros and Cons):

1) Specialization and Higher Fees - NSAs specialize in loan signings, a niche that can command higher fees per appointment compared to general notary work due to the complexity and importance of the documents involved.

2) Increasing Demand - The real estate market, despite its fluctuations, consistently requires loan signings. With the growth of refinancing and home purchasing, skilled NSAs are in demand.

3) Flexibility - Similar to mobile notaries, NSAs enjoy the flexibility of setting their schedules. This role can fit around other commitments, offering a balance between personal life and work.

4) Networking Opportunities - Working with various professionals in the real estate and financial sectors can expand your professional network, potentially leading to more business opportunities.

5) Work Variety - Each loan signing is unique, offering variety in your daily work. You'll encounter different people and visit various locations, keeping the workday interesting.

6) Certification and Training: Beyond basic notary certification, NSAs often need additional certification and training specific to loan documents, which means more time and investment upfront.

7) Irregular Income: Like many freelance or contract roles, the income can be irregular, especially in the beginning or during slow periods in the real estate market.

8) Liability Risks: Given the financial significance of the documents involved, there's a higher liability risk. Errors can have serious consequences, underlining the need for accuracy and possibly necessitating liability insurance.

9) Travel Requirements: NSAs typically travel to clients, which can lead to unpredictable work hours and additional expenses related to transportation, wear and tear on your vehicle, and time spent on the road.

10) Market Fluctuations: The demand for NSAs can be sensitive to the housing market and interest rates. Economic downturns or low refinancing rates can reduce the volume of available work.S

Meet Tamara Wiggins of Pen Point Signing Services in Virginia Beach, VA. Tamara is one of the Notary Signing agents that I trained and mentored many years ago. She started doing signings in 2012 and to date has completed more than 6,000 signings. Tamara has expanded her business to include specialty signings, and likes the freedom of being in control of her schedule. Being an NSA enabled her to get out of debt, travel, and remodel her home. Tamara is now branching out into online content creation based on healing from toxic relationships and also helps nonprofits successfully market their events on social media.

Chapter 5: Some of the More Well-Known Notary Signing Agent Companies

The following is a list of some of the more well-known companies for Certified Notary Signing Agent (CNSA) training and certification, professional associations, and signing agents companies in the country. This list does not constitute an endorsement, it should be used for reference only or as a starting point in your research.

1) National Notary Association (NNA) - the NNA has been promoting the role of notaries as trusted professionals and ensuring that they have the resources and knowledge needed to perform their duties effectively since 1957.

Headquartered in Chatsworth, California, the NNA offers a wide range of services, including notary training and certification, supplies, advocacy for notary public issues, and information on notary laws and regulations. The NNA's educational programs cover various aspects of notary work, including loan signing, and are designed to help notaries stay informed about changes in laws and best practices.

Transparency is critical for people to be able to make informed choices. On that note, the NNA along with several title companies that were fined hundreds of millions of dollars after the 2008 financial crisis, have been instrumental in the passage of signing agent requirements such as certification, and background screenings. Read more about this situation on my website at www.theresacyrus.com.

It is important to note that NO NOTARY was implicated in the 2008 financial crisis, however, mortgage lenders and title companies that made up the original consortium that the NNA was/ is a part of, HAVE been fined hundreds of millions of dollars for the part they played in the financial real estate crisis, although they have not admitted to any wrongdoing.

Also worth noting, is that the NNA which set the standards, has gone on to offer signing agent certification and background screening, so it has benefited greatly from the rules that it had a hand in setting. It's important to note that at one time, I emailed Bill Anderson, the current Vice President of Government Affairs, who has been with the NNA for many years to express my concerns. Mr. Anderson asked to speak with me, to explain their stance, and I declined.

I've been in the industry since 2001, and I've witnessed a trend of diminishing fees, greater responsibility, and liability often adding up to smaller margins. I still think that becoming a Loan Signing Agent, is an exceptional opportunity for many and worth consideration, as long as you are aware of the pros and cons of the industry.

As for the NNA, it offers a comprehensive list of notary courses, which will equip you with all the information you need to do a great job, and they are among the most affordably priced courses available. Their Certified Notary Signing Agent course is the one I took for many years.

2) Loan Signing System (LSS) - I KNOW you've seen the ads on YouTube. Around 2021, we couldn't escape seeing promotions for this company online. Founded by Mark Wills, this company provides a course for several hundred dollars. The course is much more than CNSA training, it's marketing, ongoing mentorship, and community. LSS offers a free 30-day trial to help you make an informed choice before you fully commit.

3) Notary2Pro - this company's CNSA course is among the more affordable ones. Its founder Carol Ray is a former escrow officer/ escrow office manager turned signing company owner. Notary2Pro provides mentorship as well.

Professional Notary Associations:

1) The American Society of Notaries (ASN) - founded in 1965, ASN is a non-profit company for notaries, by notaries. Their website states that the company is "the first national nonprofit association for notaries in the United States".

2) The National Notary Association (NNA) - as mentioned previously, the NNA offers resources, networking opportunities, and access to extensive training materials.

3) American Association of Notaries (AAN) - founded in 1994 in Texas, and is now nationwide. The AAN prides itself on being an advocate for strong notary laws and established teaching standards.

Signing Companies:

Signing Companies maintain a database of qualified notaries that can perform signings for their clients (that include title companies, lenders, mortgage brokers, etc.). There is often a free basic membership, and then levels of a paid membership that moves a notary up in the ranking. The higher the notary is ranked, the more visible they are, and the more likely they are to receive work. Some signing companies provide training and certifications, background screenings, and marketing assistance.

Signing companies often take a cut of the fee the client pays for the notary. For example, I had a former client that I worked with directly for more than 10 years. Several years ago, they hired a signing company. I went from being paid $125 per signing with the company, to being offered $90 for each signing through the middleman. Some people question whether the notary signing agent profession is over-saturated, others ask the same about signing companies. Following are a handful of companies that have withstood the test of time, and are highly rated by signing agents.

Some Popular Signing Companies:

1) SigningAgent.com - is an NNA company, and in all areas of the notary space, this company excels. It is very well respected in the industry and the fees it charges agents are very reasonable comparatively.

2) Notary2Pro - Notary2Pro is a notable training program for notary signing agents, offering comprehensive courses to individuals seeking certification in the field. Founded by Carol Ray, an experienced notary signing agent, Notary2Pro aims to provide top-notch training and resources to empower individuals in the loan signing industry.

3) Notary Rotary - Notary Rotary is an online platform and community for notaries public, offering a range of services, resources, and a forum for notary professionals. While I don't have specific details about its founding or location, Notary Rotary is recognized for providing a variety of tools and resources to assist notaries in their work.

4) 123Notary - is an online directory and resource platform for notaries public. It serves as a platform connecting individuals in need of notary services with qualified notaries.

5) Notary Cafe - Notary Cafe is an online platform that connects notaries with potential clients in need of notarial services. Notary Cafe allows notaries to create profiles showcasing their qualifications, services, and availability. Their online forum is a place where notaries can connect, share their experiences, and support each other

Chapter 6: Remote Online Notary (RON)

Before we dive into Remote Online Notarizations (RONs), let's compare them to In Person Electronic Notarizations (IPENs) and Remote Ink-signed Notarizations (RINs). All three are ways of performing notarial acts, but they differ in terms of the physical presence of the individuals involved and the technologies used.

In IPENs, the notary and the signer are physically present in the same location, but they use electronic tools and technology to perform the signing and notarial acts. The notary and signer must be in the same physical location, and the notary typically uses electronic signatures and seals to notarize PDF or Word documents. Traditional methods of identity verification, such as checking government-issued IDs, are still used in IPENs.

With RINs, as with RONs, the notary and signer are not physically present in the same location. In the case of RINs, the signer is communicating with the Notary Signing Agent(NSA) through a format such as Zoom, the NSA observes them signing every document, and the ones that need to be notarized are scanned and emailed, or faxed to the NSA for notarization, before they are sent back the the signer.

In RONs, the entire process is electronic. The notary and the signer are not physically present in the same location. Instead, they interact through audio-visual technology, typically using webcams and secure online platforms. RON platforms often employ advanced identity verification methods to ensure that the person appearing online is the intended signer. RONs rely on secure online platforms and electronic signatures to complete the notarial act remotely.

RONs, IPENs, and RINs all have legal and technological requirements that must be met to ensure the security and integrity of the notarial act. The acceptance and legality of these methods can vary from state to state, so it's important to be aware of and comply with the specific laws and regulations in the location where the notarization is taking place.

RONs have been around for many years in some states and were the logical next step in the digital signing landscape. Virginia was the first state to sign RONs into law back in 2011. During the COVID pandemic, however, Remote Online Notaries (RON) provided an invaluable service, verifying identities on critical documents in a variety of industries without the need to be face-to-face. RONs kept the banking and real estate industries moving at a time when America was shut down. This growing field allows a notary public to notarize documents remotely and can be a lucrative business opportunity, particularly in areas where traditional notarial services are not readily available.

As of December 31, 2023, most states have permanent RON laws but RON procedures vary from state to state, so check with your state for current rules and regulations. The states that still have temporary or no RON laws are Georgia, Mississippi, and South Carolina.

To become a RON, an individual must be a traditional notary. Some states allow you to become a traditional notary and RON simultaneously, others require you to become a conventional notary first. Generally, you must complete any RON-specific training and testing, pay any relevant fees, and secure the required insurance and bonds. RONs also need an electronic seal that takes the place of a traditional stamp/ seal, an electronic signature to replace their wet one, and they must have a digital certificate, which you can obtain from a third-party provider. The digital certificate confirms the notary's identity and can show if the completed electronic document has been tampered with.

RON procedures vary from vendor to vendor, so choosing the best RON vendor for you, one that will store your electronic records and supply any/ all tools you need to perform RONs is critical to your success. Questions to consider include: How much do their services cost? Are they fully compliant with your state? Do they provide training and support? Do they provide an electronic/ digital seal as part of what they offer, or do you provide your own?

Here are some of the companies that provide Remote Online Notarization (RON) training:

National Notary Association (NNA)

Notary2Pro

Notary Rotary

DocVerify

Many companies provide RON technology, the following companies are available in most states:

BlueNotary

OneSpan NotaryeNotaryLog LLC,

DocuSign

Pavaso

SIGNiX

NotaryCam

When considering which vendor to use for your RON business, some of the factors you might want to consider are:

1) Availability: how many states does the company service? The more, the better.

2) Costs: how much does their service cost overall (from sign up, to monthly costs)?

3) Education and/ or Support: are they available and how extensive are they?

4) Sign-up process: what are the requirements to register with their service?

5) Electronic Tools: what are the hardware and software requirements to work with the company? And do they provide any of them?

6) Electronic Records Storage: will they provide it?

7) RON Assignments: can/ will you get assignments from them?

Some Factors to Consider Before Becoming a Remote Online Notarization Provider:

1. Convenience and Accessibility - RONs offer the ultimate convenience for both notaries and clients, as documents can be notarized from virtually anywhere with internet access. This expands your potential client base beyond geographic limitations.

2. Efficiency - The process for RONs is streamlined and can save time for both notaries and their clients. Digital tools allow for quicker verification, document handling, and record-keeping.

3. Flexibility - Similar to traditional mobile notary services, RONs provide flexibility in scheduling. You can offer services outside of typical business hours, accommodating clients in different time zones or with restrictive schedules with the need for travel.

4. Growing Demand - As businesses and individuals seek more efficient, tech-savvy solutions for legal and financial processes, the demand for RON services is on the rise. This trend is likely to continue as

technology becomes more integrated into these and other sectors.

5. Environmental Benefits - RON is paperless, reducing the need for physical documents and transportation. This not only saves resources but also aligns with growing environmental sustainability efforts.

6. Technology Investment and Learning Curve - Setting up for RONs requires an initial investment in technology, including secure digital platforms certified for RON services. Notaries must also be comfortable using these technologies.

7. Legal and Regulatory Landscape - The legality and acceptance of RON vary by jurisdiction, and staying abreast of these regulations can be complex. Notaries must ensure compliance with state laws and potentially navigate varying requirements.

8. Cybersecurity Concerns - Handling sensitive documents online increases the risk of cyber threats. Notaries must implement and maintain robust security measures to guard against data breaches and ensure client confidentiality.

9. Impersonal Client Interactions - Some clients may prefer the personal touch of face-to-face interactions, which can build trust and rapport. Managing client relationships may requireadditional effort to ensure a positive experience.

Notes

Chapter 7: Wedding Officiant/ Celebrant

In the world of notary public services, officiating weddings can be an exciting and lucrative endeavor. What a romantic, profound way to make a difference in people's lives! Because at the heart of it, isn't that what entrepreneurs are doing? Being of service to others. Wedding officiants help couples seal their commitment to each other for life. The services an officiant provides can be as simple as solely officiating the wedding ceremony, or as involved as helping to plan and execute the wedding. The officiant may help the couple write their vows, select readings, and music, and may even counsel them!

Couples often seek the convenience and professionalism that a notary public can provide when it comes to tying the knot. However, the rules and regulations governing officiating a wedding vary from state to state within the United States and currently only 5 states allow notaries to perform weddings as part of their commissioned responsibilities.

1. Montana
2. Maine: must get a marriage officiant license at no extra cost
3. Nevada
4. South Carolina
5. Tennessee

Additionally, California allows a select number of specially trained notaries to issue confidential marriage certificates. You do not need to be a notary to become a wedding officiant, but being one helps you offer streamlined services that include notarization of the marriage paperwork when states allow. If you have the desire to officiate weddings, you can become a member of the Universal Life Church nondenominational church, that provides a nationally recognized online ordination.

Once you are ordained, you may choose to undergo training so that you can competently assume your role as an officiant. Typically wedding officiants' fees begin at $150 and increase according to the scope and complexity of their responsibilities.

Success as a wedding officiant notary public doesn't just depend on legal compliance; it also hinges on your ability to provide a memorable and meaningful ceremony.

Consider the Following Resources to Enhance your Skills:

1) Ceremony Scripts: Find or create wedding ceremony scripts that resonate with couples. Personalize them based on the preferences of the bride and groom.

2) Public Speaking Skills: Improve your public speaking abilities to confidently deliver ceremonies and engage the couple and their guests.

3) Networking: Build relationships with local wedding vendors, such as photographers, florists, and event planners, to gain referrals.

4) Continued Education: Stay updated on changes in marriage laws and ceremony trends.

Remember, every wedding is unique, and your role as a notary public officiant is to make the experience special for the couple. By offering professional, personalized services, you can build a successful and rewarding wedding officiation business as a notary public.

You May Want to be a Wedding Officiant if:

1) Emotional Fulfillment is Important - Officiating weddings allows you to play a key role in one of the most special and memorable days of people's lives. This can be incredibly rewarding and emotionally fulfilling.

2) Flexibility is Appealing - As a wedding officiant, you often have the flexibility to set your schedule, choose the types of ceremonies you want to conduct, and decide how many weddings you want to officiate, making it a good option for those looking for part-time, seasonal, or weekend work.

3) Diversity of Experiences Calls to you - You'll have the opportunity to meet and work with a diverse array of couples, each with their unique stories, personalities, and visions for their wedding day. This variety can make each ceremony a unique and enriching experience.

You May NOT Want to be a Wedding Officiant if:

1) Irregular Hours and Seasonality Don't Work for You - Weddings often take place on weekends and sometimes on holidays, which might conflict with personal time or other commitments. Additionally, there may be a peak wedding season, depending on your location, leading to uneven workloads throughout the year.

2) Emotional and Physical Demands Can't be met - Managing the stress and emotions of couples on their big day, along with the logistical challenges of different wedding venues, can be taxing. This role can also involve a significant amount of standing and speaking.

3) Potential for Conflict Scares You - Navigating the wishes of couples, their families, and the constraints of venues or legal requirements can sometimes lead to stressful situations or conflicts that need to be handled delicately.

Notes

Chapter 8: The World of Apostille Agents

T he US Secretary of State issues specialized certificates called apostilles to authenticate public documents, such as college diplomas, marriage certificates, and mortgage deeds so they may be used in foreign countries. Only the 156 countries (as of this writing) that are part of the Hague Apostille Convention of 1961 accept/ recognize apostilles. The country of origin is defined as where the document is coming from, and the country of destination is the foreign country it is being sent to. If a document is destined for a non-Hague country, it follows another process called legalization, and another type of authentication certificate will be needed.

Apostille agents do not need to be a notary public, however, it helps, because many of their functions, like notarizing documents and knowing what is required by the Department of State, overlap. Apostille agents serve as intermediaries between clients and the government agencies responsible for issuing apostilles. These agents possess the expertise and knowledge required to navigate the often complex process of obtaining apostilles efficiently.

The apostille acts as a coordinator or courier, helping their client navigate the process of getting the apostille, acting as a go-between for the document's issuing agency, authenticating the signature, providing translation services if necessary, and notarizing their client's signature(s) on the apostille. An apostille agent can facilitate and guide, but they cannot advise. Agents should refrain from giving legal advice or interpreting the content of the documents. Instead, focus on providing procedural guidance specific to obtaining an apostille.

Much like an Immigration Forms Specialist (see Chapter 11), an apostille agent must tread lightly to avoid the illegal practice of the law. The agent must be clear with the client about what services they can and cannot provide. Communicate that you are a notary public specializing in apostille services and not a licensed attorney.

Functions of an Apostille Agent:

As an apostille agent (much like a Permit Runner featured in Chapter 10), your primary functions include:

1) Submitting Documents - Ensuring that documents reach the appropriate government agency for apostille certification.

2) Tracking Progress - Monitoring the application status and providing updates to the client.

3) Obtaining Apostille Certificates - Collecting the apostilled documents once ready.

4) Returning Documents to Clients - Safely delivering the authenticated documents to the client.

Additional Considerations:

1) Document Translation - If documents are not in the official language of the destination country, you may need to arrange for translation services, so speaking multiple languages can be a valuable asset.

2) Clearly Define Your Role - Establish clear boundaries with your clients about what services you can and cannot offer. Avoid Offering Legal Opinions: Resist the temptation to provide input on a document's legal significance or consequences. Instead, focus on the procedural steps necessary for obtaining an apostille.

3) Stay Informed - Keep up-to-date with the latest laws and regulations related to apostilles in your jurisdiction. This knowledge will help you navigate the process without crossing into legal territory.

4) Maintain Neutrality - Refrain from taking sides or advocating for any party involved in the document. Maintain impartiality to avoid any appearance of providing legal advice.

5) Refer Complex Cases to Attorneys - If a situation goes beyond the scope of obtaining an apostille, recommend that the client seek advice from a licensed attorney.

6) Document Transactions Thoroughly - Keep detailed records of all client interactions, including copies of documents and any communication regarding the apostille process. This documents your adherence to legal and procedural boundaries.

7) E&O Insurance - Consider obtaining Errors and Omissions (E&O) insurance to provide additional protection in case you are accused of the unauthorized practice of law. While E&O insurance doesn't authorize you to practice law, it can offer some financial protection in legal disputes.

Being diligent, informed, and clear about your role as an apostille agent, helps you provide valuable services while avoiding the unauthorized practice of law. Always prioritize transparency and refer clients to legal professionals when appropriate.

Becoming an apostille agent can be a lucrative extension of your notary public business. Agents' fees vary according to the market you are in, and the job's complexity. Because your role might include delivering and/ or picking up the documents from your state's agency, a substantial amount of travel may be involved. Charging for your time, or the time of a courier is reasonable. A starting rate of $80-$150 is typical.

Special Considerations When Considering Becoming an Apostille Agent:

1) Diversity of Experiences - You'll have the opportunity to meet and work with diverse individuals, each with unique situations. This variety can make each assignment a unique and enriching experience.

2) Complexity and Responsibility - Obtaining an apostille can be complex and requires detailed knowledge of various requirements for different countries. Mistakes can have significant consequences for clients.

3) Regulatory Requirements: Understanding and keeping up to date with the legal requirements for document authentication in different jurisdictions can be challenging and time-consuming.

4) Client Stress: Clients seeking apostille services are often under time pressure or stressed about moving, working, or conducting business internationally. Managing anxious clients and ensuring that documents are processed promptly can add pressure to the role.

Chapter 9: Field Inspections (Including Collateral Inspections, Merchant Verifications and Process Serving)

Have you ever wondered what happens leading up to a car being repossessed or a property being foreclosed on? How does a business obtain a merchant account to accept credit card payments? How do you become a process server? What IS a process server? You've never wondered about any of those things? That was just me? Okay then.

But for your information, before the lender escalates to repossession or foreclosure of the collateral, they need to clarify the current situation. Does the borrower still live in the location listed? In the case of a vehicle, where is it? What kind of condition is it in? A collateral inspector who is a type of field inspector can help provide those answers.

Field inspections is an industry encompassing over 200 tasks including collateral inspections, merchant verifications, and process serving. Inspectors work in the residential mortgage, insurance, and commercial property industries and their main objective is to help clients protect an asset.

Typically, a collateral inspector will be required to inspect an asset. They will verify the asset's location, determine its condition, and upload time and date-stamped photos, and other required information to a website as needed. Usually, a series of questions will need to be answered, to complete the report for the client.

Assignments in this field can range from $10-$50 each and may not seem like much, but when you consider that you can do several (as many as 6) in an hour, it can translate to about

$150 per hour. When I first became an entrepreneur, my only source of income was loan signings. Whenever the real estate market fluctuated, I cringed. eventually, I learned not to put all my eggs in one basket. I diversified my income and gained peace of mind. My point? Every little bit counts and every paying job adds up, moving you closer to the financial goal that you've set for yourself.

With advanced training, you can move into an area like commercial insurance loss control and earn thousands of dollars per assignment. The Society of Field Inspectors (SOFI), founded in 1992, is the most well-respected organization that guides field inspectors.

Merchant Verifications: This is also a cautionary tale about how being unprofessional once, can irreparably harm a business relationship. But first, what IS merchant verification?

Any business that intends to accept credit cards must go through an approval process before they can obtain a credit card machine and have the ability to take credit cards. The approval process starts with substantiating the veracity of the business's claims about whether or not it is legitimate and operational. The payment provider will contract a neutral third party to have a field inspector who specializes in merchant verifications go out to the business to take pictures of the location, business documents (such as business license, any insurance and bank account information), and any products the business sells or inventory that it has. All of the information collected is then uploaded to the client's web portal, which is then passed on to THEIR client, to aid them in making their determination.

So on to the story of a ruined relationship...

It's about 5 pm on a weekday. I'm rushing to prepare dinner for my daughters before I leave home to get one of them off the bus, bring her back home, see that my daughters have everything they need, get them settled in bed, and then return to work.

The phone rings. It's probably not the best time to answer a call, but I've developed a Pavlovian-type response: if my phone rings, I MUST answer it, because of my fear of missing out (FOMO).

It's my client, the one I've worked with for years, one of the ones I have a great relationship with (or so I thought), and as far as I know, they have never had any issues with the quality of my work. They have the customer on the line, the one I've been unable to pin down. I received an order to verify their business and I've made numerous attempts to contact them to set up an appointment time, with no success. I am doing my best to talk with them about setting up an appointment, while multi-tasking.

At some point, I heard the customer say "See what I mean?". We finish the call, and my client later tells me they've canceled the order. I never hear from them again. I called them several times in the ensuing years to find out what happened but they never returned my call. And just like that I no longer have a client I worked with for almost 10 years, that paid me thousands and thousands of dollars.

Since I have never spoken to my former client, I am left to wonder what happened with the customer. Was my frustration at not getting hold of them becoming obvious? Did my intense focus while multitasking on the call come across as brusque and impatient? I can certainly see it from their perspective. And while I would have liked to have been given another chance, to have been given the benefit of the doubt and treated with grace and compassion, it is a client's right to sever ties with you, for whatever reason.

Similarly, it is YOUR right to end a relationship with any business that is not treating you the way you would like to be treated, OR doesn't do business in what you consider to be an ethical, integrous manner.

So let my experience serve as a warning to you. If it doesn't work for you to answer the phone, or to take an appointment at a certain time, DON'T.

What works best is to manage your business in a way that has integrity, not just for your client, but for your life as well. The temptation is to gobble up as much work as you can in pursuit of that 6 figure income, but single parents be forewarned (in fact everyone should take note), balance, being sensible with what, and how much you commit to, is imperative.

If I had to do it over again, I would have let that phone call go to voicemail and respond later when I had honored my commitments to my children. Alas, I didn't, and I was left to reckon with how I could have handled the situation better. Although my work spoke for itself, some grace and compassion would have been welcomed.

Process server: We've all seen movies where the person is just going on about their business at work, in their neighborhood, or at a restaurant, and an unknown person approaches them while calling out their name. Once they respond, they're handed an envelope and told "You've been served". That person is a process server, and they have a very important place in the judicial process. Process servers have to be calm, persistent, and patient.

When someone has been summoned to a legal proceeding, they must be informed of that fact promptly. A process server ensures that an individual is notified of the legal situation they are involved in, helping them to show up in court at the appropriate time. Once a person has been served, the process server must verify that they have delivered the legal papers, this is called an affidavit of service and is a notarized document that is returned to the entity that requested the service. Along with being a courier or messenger, a process server may also file court papers and retrieve documents. Process servers must have a valid driver's license.

Process serving is governed by state and federal law, and requirements vary from state to state and are highly regulated in the following: Alaska, Arizona, California, Florida, Georgia, Illinois, Missouri, Montana, Nevada, New York

City, Oklahoma, Texas, and Washington. Knowing the laws in your jurisdiction is key, for example, does your state allow an individual to be served on Sunday? If you decide you'd like to become a process server, the local county courthouse or state association would be a good place to start. They can tell you whether or not you need to be certified, and if you require insurance and/ or a bond.

Once you have met the requirements and have become a process server, market your services to businesses that extend credit or litigate debtors such as law offices and/ or collection agencies. A process server can earn about $100 per assignment plus travel expenses.

Richard Law co-founded SOFI with his wife Doann. The way Richard tells it is, back in the day no place listed all the competent field inspectors. When Richard lamented that there was no repository for field inspectors like himself, Doann another inspector, and Richard's future wife said "Well, why don't you create one!" Richard replied, "Why don't YOU do it!". And the rest is history. Richard, a former Navy commander, and real estate broker, as well as the owner of several other businesses, is a wealth of information and his advice is to pick the best parts of the work, don't spend time doing things you don't like and don't care for. Plus ditch the low-paying offers, they hurt everyone.

Notes

Chapter 10: Permit Runner

A permit runner is a professional service provider who assists individuals and businesses in obtaining various permits, licenses, or other legal documents from government agencies or relevant authorities. Sometimes a permit runner is also called a permit expediter, however, a permit expediter is usually more involved in the process, and therefore needs to have a much more extensive knowledge of the permitting process. A permit runner functions more in the capacity of a courier.

In other words, a permit runner acts as a liaison between a contractor or homeowner and the local government. There are classes available to learn how to become a permit runner, but generally no training or certifications are required. Check with your jurisdiction to determine what is required. If you're starting your permit-running business from scratch, and have very little to no experience, you may want to go down to your local building department and become familiar with the different types of applications and the various requirements of that agency.

Being a notary public can be an advantage. It allows you to handle notarized documents required for some permits, streamlining the process for clients and increasing your service offerings. A notary with a construction background might consider specializing in building permits, while someone familiar with the real estate industry might consider specializing in obtaining permits related to real estate transactions, business licenses, or other legal documentation on behalf of their clients.

The Function of a Permit Runner:

As a permit runner for a construction company or homeowner, their primary function involves taking completed documents from the contractor or homeowner to the building department and back. If the client is completely unfamiliar with the process, the permit runner may first need to assemble all the documents needed. Once all the necessary paperwork is filled out and signed, the completed package is taken to the building department, where a clerk reviews the paperwork for accuracy and completeness. When the paperwork is processed and uploaded, an application number is provided, which the permit runner gives to the contractor or homeowner.

As soon as the project is approved, the permit runner returns to the building department, collects the approved plans, and returns them to the contractor or homeowner. This process can also occur online, that is, instead of going to a physical building, the permit runner will go online to submit the necessary documents on their client's behalf.

A successful permit runner must excel in several key areas:

1) Submission of Applications: They need to ensure that completed applications and supporting documents are accurately submitted to the appropriate government agencies or regulatory bodies.

2) Follow-Up and Tracking: Monitoring the progress of permit applications is crucial, providing regular updates to clients to keep them informed of any developments.

3) Resolution of Issues: They should be adept at addressing any issues or discrepancies that arise during the application process, and swiftly finding solutions to ensure smooth progress.

4) Obtaining and Delivering Permits: Retrieving approved permits or licenses and promptly delivering them to clients is essential to finalize the process.

In terms of skills and qualifications:

1) Legal Knowledge: A solid understanding of the legal requirements and procedures for obtaining permits and licenses in various jurisdictions is fundamental.

2) Communication Skills: Strong communication abilities are necessary for liaising effectively with government agencies, clients, and other stakeholders involved in the process.

3) Networking: Building connections with government officials, regulatory bodies, and industry professionals can streamline the permit acquisition process, providing valuable insights and assistance when needed.

Typically, a permit runner charges between $75-$200. Fees are heavily dependent on location. If there's a lot of construction occurring in an area, and lots of new developments being built, there may be a big demand for your services, and you may be able to charge higher fees.

Prices also vary according to the distance traveled, and how much you'll be doing for your client. Is the permit runner running multiple permits? Are they putting together the entire application package for the client, because they are completely unfamiliar with the process? Some businesses hire a dedicated permit runner, those employees usually earn about $20/ hr based on information obtained from ZipRecruiter.

States Where Permit Running is Restricted:

There are no federal laws specifically governing permit running. However, some states may have specific regulations or licensing requirements for permit runners. It's essential to research and familiarize yourself with the laws in your specific jurisdiction to ensure compliance.

Ensuring Legal Compliance:

To ensure you're operating within legal boundaries as a permit runner, consider the following:

1) Stay Informed: Keep up-to-date with the latest laws and regulations related to permits and licenses in your jurisdiction.

2) Document Transactions Thoroughly: Keep detailed records of all interactions with clients, including copies of documents and any communication regarding the permit acquisition process.

3) Refer to Legal Professionals: If a situation requires legal advice or involves complex legal issues, recommend that the client consult with a qualified attorney.

4) E&O Insurance: Consider obtaining Errors and Omissions (E&O) insurance to provide an additional layer of protection in case of legal disputes.

By following these steps and maintaining a commitment to legal compliance, you can establish yourself as a trusted and effective permit runner, providing valuable services to your clients. Always prioritize transparency and professionalism in your interactions with clients and regulatory authorities.

Corixa Bran of Eli Mobile Notary and Permit Runner, has been running permits for 5 years and works with a local construction company in the Atlanta Georgia area. Corixa took an online class in Florida to become a permit runner. Typically it takes her about 8-10 hours to run 20-25 electrical and plumbing permits a week. Corixa is also a signing agent and works with her husband in his construction company as a painter. Whew! She is a side hustle queen!

When I asked Corixa if she would recommend someone get into permit running, she said "Try it! It's on your own time, there's very little stress, and if you make a mistake, you can correct it without someone breathing down your neck".

Notes

Chapter 11: Immigration Forms Specialist

T o enter and/ or file for residency in the U.S., an individual must fill out a plethora of forms that can be confusing under the best of circumstances. As per the United States Citizenship, Immigration and Services (USCIS), these forms include the I-485 (application to register permanent residence) and the N-400 (application for U.S. citizenship), N-600 (application for certificate of citizenship), I-130 (petition for alien relative) and I-864 (affidavit of support) and many others. Having a good grasp of all the forms is key in this business.

An Immigration Forms Specialist (IFS) is an individual who provides non-legal assistance to people completing immigration forms to apply for residency in the United States. Non-legal assistance includes finding and putting together the necessary forms (although the IFS cannot decide which forms to fill out), filling out the forms correctly and completely, obtaining any supporting documentation that is needed, translation services, submitting the completed document(s), and/ or making referrals if legal assistance is required. While a person doesn't need to be a lawyer to fill out the required paperwork, how well they read and write English and their ability to be detail-oriented, is critical to meet the package submission requirements.

IFSs walk a fine line between legally performing their duties, and illegally doing so. They must be clear about their roles and responsibilities and communicate them effectively to their clients so that they do not engage in the unauthorized practice of law (UPL). UPL is discussed in depth in Chapter 14. At this time, we will briefly address what are considered legal services, and therefore outside the scope of the IFS.

What an Immigrant Forms Specialist CAN'T do:

1) An IFS cannot tell a client what forms they need or don't need,

2) They cannot advise their client on how to respond to the questions on a form.

3) Explaining the immigration options available to your client is prohibited, and

4) Representing your client in court is illegal.

The title of the position may vary from state to state:

California: Immigration Consultant,
Georgia: Immigration Assistance Provider,
Illinois: Immigration Assistance Service Provider,
Maryland: Immigration Consultant,
Michigan: Immigration Clerical Assistant,
Minnesota: Immigration Assistance Provider,
Nevada: Document Preparation Services Provider,
New York: Immigration Assistance Provider, and
Utah: Immigration Consultant.

States requirements vary, but at the writing of this book, Immigration Form Specialists and other non-attorneys are allowed to provide immigration consulting or assistance services in the following states: Arizona, California, Georgia, Illinois, Maine, Maryland, Michigan, Minnesota, Nevada, New York, Oklahoma, South Carolina, Utah, and Washington.

The following states limit or forbid non-attorneys from providing immigration consultation/ assistance services in the following states, check with your state for the most up-to-date information: Arkansas, California, Colorado, Connecticut, Illinois, Iowa, Indiana, Kansas, Maine, Massachusetts, Michigan, Mississippi, Montana, Nebraska, Nevada, New Jersey, New Mexico, New York, North Carolina, North Dakota, Oklahoma, Oregon, Pennsylvania,

South Carolina, Tennessee, Texas, Utah, Virginia, Washington, West Virginia and Wisconsin.

An Immigration Forms Specialist is not allowed to perform services that an attorney or accredited representative would provide, such as explaining immigration options, giving advice about which immigration forms to use, or representing a client at an immigration hearing.

IFSs often need to have a surety bond, get licensed and/ or certified, and submit the required application to the Secretary of State. Background screening is frequently a requirement to provide this service. Immigration Forms Specialists are limited to what they can charge for certain services, for example, California limits the fee for entering the client's data into the form to $15, however, many aspects of their fee are NOT limited, such as travel, translations, etc. Ultimately the fee you can charge is based on what the market in your area can bear.

The USCIS website indicates that a record-breaking 10.9 million immigration cases were filed in 2023 and this number is expected to continue to rise, so the demand for IFSs will likely increase too. Although many states restrict how much can be charged for these services, there is still room for an IFS to grow a lucrative business.

Notes

Chapter 12: Working With the Federal Government

We will look into the world of doing business, with local, regional, state, and federal governments. The nature of the available work varies at the different levels of government. Working with the federal government is often one of the best-paying opportunities that a business can have. The US government is the largest user of goods and services in the world and pays more than $50 billion to small businesses annually to meet their needs. To engage successfully with the federal government as a business, there are several key steps and considerations to follow. Here's a simplified version of the process, along with a clear step-by-step guide:

Step-by-Step Guide to Doing Business with the Federal Government:

1) Obtain a DUNS Number - Start by securing a number from the Data Universal Numbering System (DUNS), which is necessary for federal business activities.

2) Acquire an Employer Identification Number (EIN) - This tax identification number is crucial for your business's financial operations.

3) Identify Your Industry Classification Codes - Knowing your North American Industry Classification System (NAICS) and Standard Industrial Classification (SIC) codes is necessary for completing your SAM.gov registration and identifying your industry sector.

4) Register with the System for Award Management (SAM) - Complete your registration at www.SAM.gov to become eligible to apply for federal awards. During this process, you

can self-certify your business as small or minority-owned if applicable.

5) Understand the Definition of a Small Business - The US Department of State provides guidelines on what constitutes a small business, based on employee count or average annual receipts. More information is available on their website www.state.gov.

6) Self-Certify as a Small Disadvantaged Business - If your business meets the criteria, self-certifying can give you access to a portion of the $50 billion in contracts reserved for small disadvantaged businesses.

7) Seek Certification for Special Categories - If your business is veteran-owned, service-disabled veteran-owned, located in a historically underutilized business zone (HUBZone), economically and socially disadvantaged, or woman-owned, consider applying for specific certifications like the Vets First Verification Program, HUBZone, and 8(a) to enhance your eligibility for certain contracts.

8) Register with the General Services Administration (GSA) Multiple Award Schedule - This registration increases your chances of obtaining government contracts across various agencies.

9) Explore Contracting Opportunities - With all registrations complete, you can now search for contracting opportunities through Federal Business Opportunities (FedBizOpps).

Pros and Cons to Consider in Doing Business With the Federal Government:

Pros: 1) Stable Revenue Source - Federal contracts can provide a stable and reliable source of revenue. The government is a large customer that requires a wide variety of goods and services regularly.

2) Large-Scale Opportunities - The federal government offers contracts that can be significantly larger than those available in the private sector, potentially leading to substantial business growth.

3) Set-Aside Contracts - The government sets aside a certain percentage of contracts specifically for small businesses, including those owned by women, veterans, and minorities, to help them compete on a level playing field.

4) Payment Reliability - The federal government is known for being a reliable payer, although payment cycles can be longer than in the private sector. Laws such as the Prompt Payment Act ensure that payments are made promptly.

5) Public Sector Experience - Working with the federal government can enhance your company's credentials and reputation, making your business more attractive to other clients, both public and private.

Cons: 1) Complex Bidding Process - The process of bidding for government contracts can be complex and time-consuming, requiring a significant amount of paperwork and adherence to strict guidelines.

2) Regulatory Compliance - Government contracts come with stringent regulatory requirements that can be burdensome for small businesses to meet and maintain over time.

3) Slow Procurement Cycle - The time from bidding on a contract to the commencement of work can be lengthy, which might strain your business's operational planning and cash flow.

4) Potential for Increased Scrutiny - Doing business with the government means adhering to higher standards of transparency and accountability, including possible audits and monitoring of your operations and financials.

5) Intense Competition - Despite set-asides, the competition for government contracts is still intense, including from larger businesses that have more experience, resources, and dedicated teams for navigating the procurement process.

6) Requires a Financially Sound Business - Getting the contract is just the beginning. Since you won't receive all the money at once, you must be able to budget the money you have until the next payout.

Opportunities and Support:

1) The Department of Defense (DoD) is notably the largest purchaser of goods and services from small businesses, but other agencies such as US Immigration and Customs Enforcement (USICE), also contract notary services independently.

2) Support for Small Businesses - If the process seems daunting, Procurement Technical Assistance Centers (PTACs) offer guidance. These centers are often attached to colleges and universities in your area, and provide free or low-cost assistance to businesses wanting to sell to the government. Locate your nearest PTAC at https://www.dla.mil/Small-Business/Pages/ptap/.

By following these steps and utilizing available resources, notaries and entrepreneurs can effectively navigate the complexities of doing business with the federal government, positioning themselves to take advantage of significant contracting opportunities. We have barely scratched the surface of this opportunity, which may be the most lucrative of all the opportunities featured in this book. Start with the information you've been given here, explore SAM.gov, and watch the many videos on YouTube that go into the topic more deeply.

Monica Wilder is the founder of Notary Nerds University, an online training platform. Monica is a mortgage broker who was initially looking for a way to supplement her income so that any transactions that didn't go through, didn't impact her bottom line. Once she got into the loan signing agent space, she realized it wasn't for her… and more importantly, she realized that the education and training space is where her heart is. After almost 3 years in that business, she is thriving and helping many others to thrive as well. On the day I talked to her, she was excitedly completing a bid for a government contract worth hundreds of thousands of dollars and was enjoying the process.

Notes

Chapter 13: Other Possibilities (Exam Proctor, and Finger print Technician)

Exam Proctor:

An exam proctor is someone who oversees an exam from start to finish and monitors students in person or online to ensure academic integrity. Proctoring can be fully human-assisted, OR a hybrid of human and artificial intelligence (AI).

If the student(s) is being monitored online, a webcam and microphone-enabled laptop or desktop, a reliable internet connection, and an updated internet browser are essential.

While an exam proctor doesn't necessarily need to be a notary, the fact that notaries are background screened makes them an ideal candidate for this type of assignment. Smarterproctoring.com, which provides proctors, requires proctors to "hold a current professional position such as educator, notary, librarian, government employee, military personnel, business professional, etc".

Individuals typically earn $25-30 per hour to proctor an exam. Notaries interested in becoming exam proctors can browse the web for other proctoring companies.

Finger Printing Services:

This business is an obvious and natural extension of notarial services, even though it is not a notarial act and may be regulated by law. The places that need fingerprinting services are wide-ranging and include law enforcement, hospitals, financial organizations, childcare services, and insurance services, to name a few.

Fingerprinting fees start at about $50 and increase up to about $200 based on several factors like distance traveled, whether you're using fingerprint cards or a fingerprint scanner.

There are currently no state or federal requirements for becoming a fingerprinting provider or technician.

Chapter 14: Unauthorized Practice of Law (UPL)

The unauthorized practice of law (UPL) is defined as the offering of legal services, such as drafting legal documents, giving legal advice, or representing an individual in legal proceedings without having the proper licenses to do so.

Attorneys (lawyers) are licensed to provide these services in the jurisdiction(s) in which they operate. Notaries are ministerial officers and as such have very limited powers, unlike lawyers who are judicial officials, and have much greater authority under the law. A notary that is being supervised by a lawyer, may have the ability to draft legal documents.

As a notary public, it's crucial to be aware of the boundaries of your role to avoid unintentionally crossing into the realm of legal practice. Engaging in UPL can result in serious consequences, both legally and professionally. If a notary is found guilty of UPL, they can be fined, imprisoned, and have their notary commission revoked.

Being accused of UPL can tarnish your reputation within the legal and notary communities, making it difficult to rebuild trust. You may also be held liable for any harm or financial losses suffered by clients due to your unauthorized legal advice or services.

How to Avoid Unauthorized Practice of Law:

To steer clear of UPL, follow these guidelines:

1) Know Your Role - Understand the specific duties and limitations of a notary public. Your primary function is to witness and authenticate signatures, not provide legal advice.

2) Communicate Your Role - Immediately communicate your role to your clients to avoid confusion. Reiterate your

role as often as needed. If a client is not willing to respect your boundaries, refrain from doing business with them.

3) Refer to Legal Professionals - If a situation requires legal expertise, always recommend that individuals consult with a qualified attorney, the loan officer, the title agent, or other professional you've been contracted to represent. Avoid giving legal opinions or interpreting documents beyond your notarial duties.

4) Maintain Neutrality - Stay impartial and refrain from taking sides in legal matters. Your role is to ensure that documents are properly executed, not to advocate for any party.

5) Avoid Preparing Legal Documents - Resist the temptation to draft or prepare legal documents. Leave this task to licensed attorneys. You can complete a document on behalf of a client (such as in the role of an Immigration Forms Specialist (see Chapter 11)), but you cannot create it.

6) Stay Informed - Keep up-to-date with notary laws and regulations in your jurisdiction to ensure you're operating within legal boundaries.

7) Seek Continuing Education - Consider participating in legal education courses or workshops designed for notaries. These can help the notary stay informed about legal issues without engaging in UPL.

8) Purchase Errors and Omissions (E&O) Insurance - E&O insurance can provide an additional layer of protection in case you're accused of UPL, though it does not authorize you to practice law.

Notaries play a crucial role in the legal system, but they need to be aware of the boundaries of their authority to avoid the unauthorized practice of law.

Here are some resources available for notaries to help them stay within their legal limits:

1) State Notary Regulating Agencies - Each state in the U.S. has a notary regulating agency that provides guidelines and resources for notaries. These agencies often have information on what notaries can and cannot do in their respective states.

2) National Notary Association (NNA) - The NNA provides educational resources and training for notaries, including guidance on avoiding the unauthorized practice of law.

3) American Society of Notaries (ASN) - Similar to the NNA, the ASN offers educational materials and resources for notaries, including information on best practices and legal limitations.

4) Legal Seminars and Workshops - Many organizations, including notary associations and law firms, offer seminars or workshops specifically designed to educate notaries on legal boundaries.

5) Online Forums and Communities - Participating in online forums or communities for notaries can be a great way to learn from experienced notaries and get advice on how to handle different situations.

6) Notary Journals and Recordkeeping Guides - Proper record-keeping is essential for notaries. Many organizations and supply companies offer journals and guides that help notaries keep accurate records of their notarial acts.

7) State Statutes and Regulations - Familiarize yourself with your state's notary laws and regulations. They should clearly outline what you can and cannot do as a notary.

8) Legal Consultation - If a notary encounters a situation that is unclear or potentially involves the practice of law, seeking legal advice or consulting an attorney is always a good idea.

Remember, while notaries can provide valuable services, they must always operate within the bounds of their legal authority. If a situation involves giving legal advice or performing tasks that require legal expertise, it's best to consult a licensed attorney.

Chapter 15: Tax Advantages of Owning a Business

How would you like to increase your earnings by as much as 30%? Well, that's the value that tax deductions can provide. While a W-2/wage earner cannot recoup their mileage expenses for traveling to and from their job, or for a designated room or area in their home used for remote work, an entrepreneur can!

We can deduct a portion of our electric, gas, water, and internet bills, based on the square footage that we use exclusively for business. For example, if my home is 1000 square feet (sq. ft.), and I use either a 200 sq. ft. room or a portion of a room measuring 20 sq. ft., I can deduct a percentage - ranging from 20% to 2% based on the bills in the scenarios mentioned previously. These amounts add up!

For those of us who drive a lot for your business, as long as we can prove that we use our vehicle for business, we can claim a standard deduction for the miles we drove, OR we can itemize all of our related expenses including maintenance such as gas and tires, insurance, registration, car wash membership, and repairs.

As entrepreneurs, we can expense our equipment, including our laptop, desktop computer, printer, and cell phone (if used exclusively for business), or a portion of the cell phone bill if we can verify it was used for work. We can deduct certain meals, the cost to obtain our notary license, stamp, seal, and journal, E&O insurance, certifications, background screening, printer ink, and copy/ print paper, You can even deduct THIS BOOK, the list goes on! Effectively, this enables us to get some of our money back, or at the very least, to offset some of the taxes we owe. Does this information light you up as much as it lights me up?!

The Internal Revenue Service (I.R.S.) has stringent rules about what a business owner can or cannot deduct, so contact a tax professional for advice on the deductions you intend to claim, and always err on the side of caution!

Chapter 16: What's Next?

The steps to establish many, if not all, of the businesses referred to in this book, are similar. If your objective is to pursue the business without becoming a notary, simply skip the first 3 steps:

1) **Become a Notary Public**: Your journey starts with becoming a notary public. Requirements vary by state, but they usually include completing an application, passing an exam, and paying a fee.

1) **Meet State Requirements:** Some states may have additional requirements, such as background checks or specific training. Make sure you comply with all state regulations.

3) **Obtain Notary Supplies:** You'll need essential supplies, including a notary stamp, seal, journal, and errors and omissions insurance (and a surety bond if necessary in your field).

4) **Training:** Consider taking a training course. Many reputable organizations offer online or in-person training programs that cover the nuances of the business you're creating, and its best practices.

5) **Build a Professional Profile:** Create a professional online presence to market your services. A well-designed website and active social media profiles can help potential clients find you. You can find a professional on Fiverr at almost any budget to help you develop your website or social media profiles.

6) **Advertise Your Services:** Reach out to local companies to let them know about your services. For example, if you're creating a loan signing business, contact real estate agents,

mortgage brokers, and title companies in your area or region. Networking is key in this industry.

Optimize your website for Search Engine Optimization (SEO). Use relevant keywords, quality content, meta descriptions, tags, alt text on images, etc. to help drive organic traffic from search engines.

Leverage social media. Create FREE business pages on platforms like Facebook, Instagram, Twitter, etc. Post engaging content daily/weekly and interact with followers.

Run targeted Facebook and Instagram ads. Create highly-targeted, low-budget ads to reach your ideal audience. Aim for conversions, not just reach. Conversions are specific actions that you want e.g. buy my book, as opposed to reach which simply targets as many people as possible.

Claim and update free business listings. Register with Google My Business, Yelp, TripAdvisor, etc. Keep information accurate and respond to reviews.

Start a blog. Publish 4-8 educational, entertaining blog posts per month to attract and retain website visitors. Embed calls-to-action.

Guest post on industry blogs. Pitch relevant blogs in your industry to write posts for added exposure and backlinks.

Launch email marketing. Collect emails to build an audience to promote to. Send quality content on a regular schedule.

Partner with influencers. Collaborate on sponsored posts, product giveaways, reviews, etc. in exchange for exposure.

Distribute promotional materials. Business cards, flyers, postcards, coupons, samples, etc. Be strategic with placement.

7) **Set Your Prices:** Research industry standards in your area to determine competitive pricing for your deliverables. Fees may vary based on the complexity of the job you're doing and the demand for what you offer in your area.

8) **Stay Updated:** Keep up with changes in regulations, forms, and industry trends. Continuous learning is essential to maintain your credibility and professionalism.

Notes

Chapter 17: Supplies and Requirements

Fortunately, many of us already have some, if not all, of the commonly used tools for the businesses highlighted in this book. Most of us already have a smartphone, a laptop and/ or desktop computer, a high-speed internet connection, and a laser printer. The printer should have 2 paper trays: one for legal paper (8.5"x14") and one for letter paper (8.5"x11"). That's it.

In many cases, this is all that is needed to start your business once you've obtained your notary license, and have your stamp, seal, notary journal, and Errors and Omissions Insurance.

Notary Stamp:

The main recommendation I have regarding this item is SIZE. Size DOES matter in this instance, and the smaller your stamp is (as long as it is still legible) the better it is. Often the size of the area available for you to put your stamp is minuscule. So, stamps that are about 2 inches x .5 inches are better. Much smaller and the clarity of the information on your stamp begins to become impaired. Self-inking stamps are preferred since they reduce the mess that can be caused.

The Guardian of Integrity: The Notary Journal

In the realm of notarial duties, meticulous record-keeping is more than a formality—it's a cornerstone of trust, integrity, and accountability. The notary journal stands as a silent witness to each transaction, preserving a comprehensive record of every notarized act. Let us explore the significance of the notary journal, what it entails, and why it's indispensable for every notary public.

What is a Notary Journal?

A notary journal, also known as a notary logbook or notary record, is a bound, chronological record that a notary public uses to document every notarial act performed. It serves as an organized repository of vital information, providing an unbiased account of the parties involved, the type of document notarized, and other pertinent details.

Types of Notary Journals:

Traditional Paper Journals:

These are physical, bound books with pre-printed pages specifically designed for notary entries. They typically include columns for recording essential information like date, time, type of document, names of signers, and their identification details.

Electronic Notary Journals:

With advancements in technology, electronic notary journals have gained popularity. These digital versions offer the same functionalities as traditional paper journals but allow for easy search, storage, and retrieval of notarial records. They also often come with added security features to protect sensitive information.

Why Does a Notary Need a Journal:

1) Legal Compliance and Accountability: - A notary journal is more than just a record-keeping tool—it's a legal requirement in many jurisdictions. Maintaining an accurate and complete journal is essential for demonstrating compliance with state laws and regulations governing notarial acts. It serves as a tangible record of due diligence, providing a layer of protection in case of legal disputes.

2) Evidence of Notarial Acts - A well-maintained notary journal is a critical piece of evidence in case the validity of a notarized document is ever challenged. It acts as an impartial witness, substantiating the authenticity of the transaction, the

identity of the parties involved, and the notary's adherence to proper procedures.

3) Protection Against Fraud and Misconduct - The notary journal acts as a safeguard against fraudulent activities or misconduct. In the unfortunate event that a notarized document is involved in a fraudulent scheme, a detailed journal entry can aid in identifying the responsible parties and holding them accountable.

4) Professionalism and Credibility - Beyond legal requirements, maintaining a notary journal demonstrates a commitment to professionalism and integrity. It shows clients and colleagues that you take your role as a notary public seriously and are dedicated to upholding the highest standards of ethical conduct.

In the end, the notary journal is a time-honored guardian of trust, accountability, and integrity in the notarial profession. Whether in the form of a traditional paper journal or a digital record-keeping system, its importance cannot be overstated. By faithfully maintaining a comprehensive notary journal, you're not only adhering to legal obligations but also cementing your reputation as a trustworthy and responsible notary public.

Background checks/ screenings:

A background check is a process of investigating and compiling a person's criminal, financial, and sometimes employment history. It is commonly used by companies and organizations when hiring individuals for sensitive positions or roles that involve a level of trust and responsibility. As far as notaries and loan signing agents are concerned, companies often require background checks for several reasons:

1) Legal Requirements - Many jurisdictions have legal requirements or regulations regarding the eligibility criteria for becoming a notary public or a loan signing agent. These requirements may include a clean criminal record, absence of certain convictions, and good moral character. Companies

may conduct background checks to ensure that the individuals they hire meet these legal standards.

2) Client Trust - Notaries and loan signing agents handle important and often confidential documents, including financial and legal paperwork. Companies want to assure their clients that the individuals they send for notarization or loan signings are trustworthy and have a clean background.

3) Risk Mitigation - Conducting background checks helps companies identify potential risks associated with hiring a notary or loan signing agent. This includes assessing the risk of fraud, embezzlement, or other unethical behavior that could be detrimental to the company or its clients.

4) Compliance with Industry Standards - Some industries, especially those related to finance and real estate, may have industry standards or best practices that recommend or require background checks for individuals handling sensitive transactions.

5) Insurance Requirements - Companies may have insurance policies in place that require them to ensure the reliability and integrity of individuals providing notary or loan signing services. A background check can be a component of this risk management process.

Notaries and loan signing agents need to be aware of and compliant with the background check requirements in their jurisdiction. Additionally, they should be prepared to undergo background checks when working with companies that contract their services, as it is a common practice to ensure the credibility and trustworthiness of individuals in these roles.

Errors and Omissions Insurance:

In the world of notaries, entrepreneurs, and aspiring business owners, success often hinges on trust and reliability. However, no matter how diligent and meticulous you are in your business endeavors, there's always a chance that something could go awry. This is where Errors and

Omissions (E&O) insurance comes in as a crucial safeguard, offering protection against potential pitfalls that may arise in the course of your professional journey.

What is E&O Insurance?

Errors and Omissions (E&O) insurance, also known as professional liability insurance, is a specialized type of coverage designed to protect individuals and businesses from financial losses arising due to alleged professional errors, omissions, or negligence. For notaries, entrepreneurs, and aspiring business owners, E&O insurance is an essential shield that provides peace of mind and financial security.

Why is E&O Insurance Needed?

1) Legal Safeguard -In the fast-paced world of business, mistakes can happen, no matter how careful one is. Even the most diligent professionals can find themselves facing legal action due to alleged errors, omissions, or oversights in their services. Without E&O insurance, these legal battles can result in substantial financial losses and, in some cases, jeopardize the very existence of your business.

2) Maintaining Trust and Credibility -When you invest in E&O insurance, you're demonstrating a commitment to professionalism and accountability. This reassures your clients that you take their interests seriously and are willing to back your services with a solid financial safety net. This level of transparency and dedication builds trust, which is invaluable for any business seeking long-term success.

To illustrate the importance of E&O insurance, consider the following hypothetical scenario:

Meet Sarah, a notary public with a thriving business. One day, Sarah is entrusted with handling an important real estate transaction, where she is responsible for verifying signatures and notarizing the necessary documents. Due to a momentary lapse in concentration, Sarah overlooks a critical signature, and by the time the omission is discovered and corrected, the loan is not able to be funded on schedule, plus the interest rate lock has expired! The borrower incurs late charges and penalties AND now has to pay thousands of dollars MORE because of the higher interest rate they may now be forced to accept. The frustrated parties involved decide to take legal action against Sarah, seeking compensation for the financial losses incurred due to the delay.

Without E&O insurance, Sarah could find herself facing a potentially devastating financial burden. Legal fees, settlement costs, and potential damages could mount up quickly, threatening the stability of her business and her finances.

However, with an adequate E&O insurance policy in place, Sarah can breathe a sigh of relief. Her insurance policy covers the legal expenses, ensuring that her business remains intact, and her reputation remains intact. This illustration serves as a powerful reminder of the invaluable protection that E&O insurance offers to notaries, entrepreneurs, and aspiring business owners.

Several companies provide E&O insurance, but not all are created equal. Check notary message boards such as the Notary Cafe Forum, to gain some insight into companies before making your choice. The National Notary Association offers E&O insurance from Merchants Bonding Company, this is the insurance that I have had for my entire notarial career. Be sure to do your due diligence to source the company that works best for you.

Printer:

Loan Signing Agents (and several of the other businesses featured), will need a high-quality multi-function laser fax/ scan/ copy printer with dual trays that can duplex print, has large paper capacity, and wireless printing capability. Most of my printers have been the Brother brand, however, I have also used Epson, HP, and Canon printers.

This may be a bit controversial, but I do not recommend having a mobile setup, at least not in the beginning. My intention is to help you start a business affordably. In many if not all the cases in this book, you can build a very profitable business, and satisfy your clientele with very few pieces of equipment: a smartphone, laptop, and laser printer (like the one listed above). Everything else is cool, but not strictly essential.

And while you may choose to have a mobile setup if you're an LSA, consider the consequences of being readily available all the time. Clients will treat you how you teach them to, and if you make it a habit to being available all the time, there is little incentive to do their best and be impeccable with their work. Accepting last-minute assignments or incomplete or incorrect packages, sets unhealthy expectations, and can lead to an overly demanding, and stressful business relationship.

Smartphone:

It is unnecessary to have the latest and the greatest. There will be plenty of time to upgrade when your business has grown and is consistently generating income. For now, it is sufficient to have a capable device, one that functions properly, has good connectivity, and has great battery life. If you're going to be traveling a lot, being able to access your phone's GPS is critical and that's one of the places where the connectivity and battery life are important. Also, make your that your phone has enough memory to do common tasks like taking quality photos and scans of documents. Make sure that your charging cables are in good working condition, and have backups as needed.

Laptop/ Desktop:

For most of my business life. I used a desktop at home, and a laptop on the go (with a mobile hotspot on my phone). You may choose to integrate a tablet and hotspot device, the choice is up to you. Again, in the beginning, only a desktop or laptop at your home office is necessary. Later on, you can add as many enhancements as you see fit.

Paper Shredder:

Part of your responsibility is to protect your client's privacy. Having a well-equipped cross-cut paper shredder that can handle large amounts of paper, including staples and clips will help you do that. The average loan package is about 150 pages including a borrower's copy, that's a lot of paper to shred if a signing is canceled for any reason and the documents have already been printed! Investing in a high-quality shredder that will do the job quickly and efficiently is key to making the most of your time and energy.

Chapter 18: Empowering Yourself for Lasting Success

C ongratulations on reaching the final chapter of Profitable Businesses for Notaries, Entrepreneurs, and Entrepreneur Wannabes!

By now, you've explored various business opportunities and learned about leveraging your notary license to create a thriving enterprise with little to no startup costs. You may have an idea about which of these businesses you'd like to develop for yourself. You may have even created a road map for yourself: you'll start with one of the businesses, develop it, and over time grow OTHER complimentary businesses with it because you want to leverage your notary license and have a variety of income streams to draw from.

But before you do ANYTHING, I want to talk to you about your mindset. If you're reading this book, you have a desire to be an architect of your destiny. Some may say that I'm being dramatic, but I don't think so. Some people are content being employees, and make no mistake employees are valuable and very much needed in our society.

However, I believe that entrepreneurs are the life force of our economy. It takes a particular type of individual to be self-employed. It takes someone courageous, committed, and somewhat comfortable with risk. The entrepreneurial journey is a beautiful one, oftentimes rewarding, exciting, and a great confidence builder. But being your own boss can also be exhausting, scary, and unproductive at times (it may take you a while to start generating the amount you money that you want or need).

Your level of success in this, or any other business endeavor, is not solely dependent on external tools and strategies. Rather your success is directly related to your ability and willingness to learn and grow from any lessons you experience. Your success is also related to your willingness to cultivate a mindset that is aligned with prosperity, worthiness, and abundance. What do you tell yourself about your ability to succeed? What do you tell yourself about your ability to make, keep, and grow money?

By addressing these internal dialogues and transforming any old, played-out mental tapes into empowering beliefs, you will set the stage for long-term benefit and fulfillment from the knowledge gained in this book.

This chapter is meant to be an introduction to a topic that is a lifelong endeavor.

Self-awareness and work style assessment:

Many of the businesses featured in Profitable Businesses have overlapping skill sets. However, for some of the businesses, being organized and detail-oriented is more important, while others need someone who can deliver under hard and fast deadlines. Some of the businesses are better suited to introverts, and some are definitely more suited to extroverts. Knowing where your strengths lie is crucial to your entrepreneurial success. I found that while I enjoy being around people, I enjoy being by myself much more, so I chose businesses where I got to work by myself most of the time (like writing this book!).

There are MANY assessment tests available to help you become more self-aware. Some of them include the more well-known ones like Myers-Briggs, Enneagram, and The Big Five personality test. The Big Five personality test is free online.

Cultivating a Success Mindset

Your mindset plays a significant role in determining your success. The thoughts and beliefs you hold about your capabilities shape your actions and outcomes. Embrace a growth mindset and cultivate self-confidence by affirming your skills, knowledge, and abilities. Continuously reminding yourself that you are fully capable of achieving greatness, and that the effort you invest will yield remarkable results.

Embracing Worthiness and Deservedness

One of the greatest obstacles to success is a sense of unworthiness or a feeling that you don't deserve prosperity. Understand that you are deserving of abundance, success, and financial well-being. Embrace your inherent worthiness and let go of any self-imposed limitations that hinder your progress. Believe that you have every right to create a prosperous business and live a fulfilling life.

Seeking Abundance in All Areas

True success encompasses more than just financial gain. It encompasses fulfillment in all aspects of life, including relationships, health, and personal growth. Open yourself up to the abundance that surrounds you and strive for balance in all areas. By nurturing a holistic approach to success, you will create a foundation for sustained happiness and prosperity.

Continuous Learning and Growth

Remember, the journey toward success is an ongoing process. Commit yourself to lifelong learning, both within your field and in personal development. Stay curious, seek new opportunities, and adapt to changes in the marketplace. Embrace challenges as learning experiences and fuel for growth. By remaining open-minded and adaptable, you will continuously expand your horizons and unlock new levels of achievement.

Rewriting Your Financial Story

Take a moment to reflect on your current relationship with money. When you read the word MONEY, what are your thoughts? "Money doesn't grow on trees", "Money is the root of all evil", "I don't have any", "I don't have enough", "I want more!". How do you FEEL in your body? Are you relaxed, or did your shoulders and gut tighten? What are the negative or limiting beliefs about money that hold you back?

Recognize that the stories we tell ourselves about money shape our financial reality. To achieve lasting success, it is crucial to rewrite your financial story by embracing thoughts of abundance, wealth, and prosperity. Forgive your missteps (real or perceived). The past is the past, there is nothing you can do about it. Your ability to release any guilt or shame around your mistakes, is directly related to your ability to succeed. Visualize yourself as a successful notary entrepreneur, thriving in your business, and attracting lucrative opportunities. FEEL the feelings of abundance, satisfaction, accomplishment, gratitude, joy, and peace that success in your business brings.

Travel With People Who Are Going There:

And you will get there too… this is an old Buddhist saying. I do not believe that we can be successful alone. I believe we need a community of like-minded individuals who will challenge and inspire us to be our best selves. Whether this community is in person or online is largely irrelevant. What matters most is that we participate in it committedly and consistently.

In conclusion, building a profitable notary business or any other venture requires more than just practical tools and techniques. It necessitates a transformation from within, addressing disempowering internal conversations about finances, money, success, abundance, worthiness, and deservedness. By embracing an empowering mindset, rewriting your financial story, and cultivating a sense of worthiness, you lay the groundwork for long-term success. Remember, success is not an overnight phenomenon but a journey of continuous growth and discovery.

As you embark on your entrepreneurial path, armed with everything you gained from this book, hold onto the belief that you are capable, deserving, and ready to achieve extraordinary success. The tools are within your reach, and now, it's time to unleash your full potential. Trust in yourself, take inspired action, and embrace the boundless possibilities that await you.

Wishing you abundant success and fulfillment on your journey!

Reading Resources

I could go on and on, there are so many good books that I've read through the years. And, if you're NOT a reader, become one! Nothing works better to expand your mind! The Psychology of Achievement by Brian Tracy (this is the one that started it all! This series of cassette tapes, blew my mind at 19 years old)

Your Money or Your Life - Vicki Robin and Joe Dominguez

EVERY BOOK by Brené Brown
Secrets of The Millionaire Mind - T. Harv Eker
Who Moved My Cheese - Dr. Spencer Johnson
Think and Grow Rich - Napoleon Hill
The Magic of Thinking Big - David Schwartz
Rich Dad Poor Dad - Robert Kiyosaki
I Will Teach You How to Be Rich - Ramit Sethi
Total Money Makeover - Dave Ramsey (and Financial Peace University class)
Start With Why - Simon Sinek
The Four-Hour Workweek - Tim Ferriss
Live Rich Die Broke - Stephen Pollan

If I had to pick just one book, I would choose Secrets of the Millionaire Mind by T Harv Eker.

That book and his Millionaire Mindset and Enlightened Warrior weekend caused a seismic shift in my relationship with money. If you read that book several times and wholeheartedly do the exercises it contains, you will transform your financial mindset.

Personal Growth and Training Development Programs like The Landmark Forum were invaluable in helping me uncover my blind spots (those things that EVERYONE could see about me, that I couldn't see about myself, that stood in the way of my success).

Also, YouTube is chuck filled with great content. Some of my favorites are Marie TV, Lisa Bilyeu, The Tim Ferriss Podcast, Diary of a CEO with Stephen Bartlett, and The Rich Roll Podcast. Codie Sanchez talks about business in a way that is both inspiring and informative... it's downright sexy! There is also abundant content on all the businesses I featured in this book. There's enough to make you an expert in each area, so DIVE IN. It's a great time to be alive. All the information and resources are at your fingertips! Remember to check out my website www.TheresaCyrus.com for periodically updated information.

You Got This!

About The Author

Theresa Cyrus is a 30-year entrepreneur, author, and educator whose mission is to make business ownership accessible to everyone—especially those who are overlooked or underestimated. As founder of The Pereleong Group LLC, she has completed thousands of real estate closings as a Certified Notary Signing Agent and helped professionals build sustainable, purpose-driven income streams.

Through her workshops, speaking engagements, and published works, Theresa blends practical strategies with mindset mastery, guiding readers and students to move from ideas to action with clarity and courage.

Her book, Profitable Businesses for Notaries, Entrepreneurs, and Entrepreneur Wannabes, reflects a lifetime of experience and a heart for service—showing how entrepreneurship can be both profitable and profoundly meaningful.

Thank You for Reading and Review Request

I hope this book has sparked new ideas and inspired you to take the next step in your business journey.

If you found it valuable, would you take a moment to leave an honest review where you purchased it?

Your feedback helps others discover the book, fuels future editions created to serve you even better, AND helps independent authors like me.

With gratitude,

Theresa

www.ingramcontent.com/pod-product-compliance
Lightning Source LLC
Chambersburg PA
CBHW052141270326
41930CB00012B/2976